The Color of Culture II

IMPACT COMMUNICATIONS

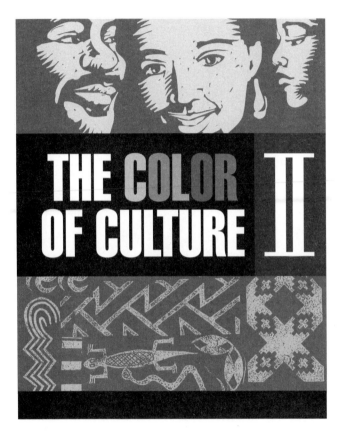

THE COLOR OF CULTURE II

Mona Lake Jones

The Color of Culture II

Library of Congress Catalogue number 96-94792
ISBN: 0-9635605-8-1

Manufactured in the United States of America

All of the poems and phrases featured in
The Color of Culture II are the original
work of Mona Lake Jones

Cover Design and Illustration by Gable Design Group
Text Design by Vic Warren, Turning Heads, Inc.

I dedicate this book to my father,
Sylvester James Lake,
who first introduced me to the beauty of words
and along with my mother, Pauline,
instilled my sense of cultural pride.

The Color of Culture II

Culture II

. . . culture is also contagious. At first it was thought only to be transmitted through families with one generation turning to pass it to the next. Now we know we can catch it from living in certain locations of the world, a particular community, neighborhood, or even from a close friend. It usually has a slow onset and needs prolonged exposure, but culture is wonderful to acquire!

Those who realize they have it often celebrate and revel in it because culture is a treasure that makes you a richer human being. Some few insulate themselves, become resistant and unaffected by any other culture and hardly recognize the one they have. They miss a whole lot of living!

The folks who have been more vulnerable to culture still have the same basic needs as others to survive and thrive, but culture changes your ability to enjoy life. Appreciation for others is enhanced, days may be happier, nature's beauty more vivid, and I could be wrong, but it seems easier to find humor in what some think to be very serious subjects.

Did I mention you can catch it just by being a certain color?

Mona Lake Jones

Catching the color of culture is like being showered by the water that has just come through a rainbow!

The best thing ever designed was the people machine
Do you remember the inventor's name?

Rotations

Consider if you may
That only for a day

Just to be amused
The colors were confused

Say on Monday all the Whites in the town
Would become Brown

The Reds would turn Black without any choice
And as Browns became Yellow they would be given no voice

And nothing could be said
When Blacks changed to Red

Not a question could be raised about whether it was right
When those who were Yellow turned out to be White

Now assume that things were going so fine
The director in charge had a change of mind

So by the time Saturday was due to arrive
Instead of one color, each would have been five

Friday, people would be back to their original skin
Just in time for a meeting to begin

On the weekend all would be required to talk and confer
To discuss what had happened and how things really were

Suppose, just suppose what the outcome could be!

It is hard to know just how to live
How much should I take
And what should I give?

Happy Day

Squeeze the day
and wring it out good
Get every drop of living
you think you should

Twist each minute
making sure not to lose
There must not be a single drop of joy
that you neglect to use

Warm by the sun rays
shining from above
Suck in all the sweet aromas
and wrap yourself in love

Dance, sing,
write a line or two
Relish in the comfort of the old
and be surprised by something new

Put your smile on first thing in the morning
and wear it all day long
Look only for the best
and find no fault or wrong

Embrace the day, hug it hard
and barely let it slip away
Then rest so you will be ready
for another happy day!

It was a long time before I realized everybody's Grandma
didn't bake sweet potato pies and play the blues

Love in the Kitchen

It wasn't the greens simmering on the stove, the smell of canned strawberry jam or the pies cooling on the counter top.
It wasn't even the gravy being stirred to pour over the mashed potatoes. It was love that filled our kitchen!

The kitchen was so full of love you could taste it when you licked the mixing spoon. You could feel it through the hot pads when you took the cornbread from the oven. You could see it on the faces sitting around the kitchen table. Love was the food being blessed and the sound of laughter when somebody told even a half-way funny story.

Folks didn't just cook in the kitchen. They hugged and cried there. Broken hearts and cut fingers were mended right in the kitchen. Over the kitchen sink was a place to show off if you could sing, and many a dance step was tried while waiting for what was being baked to turn the right color brown.

Everybody in the family came through the kitchen to get a helping of love. Company would get enough love to take some home with them. There was hardly any left over because somebody was always coming back for seconds.

Sometimes if you needed a refill of love, you could just go sit in the kitchen all by yourself, close your eyes, and help yourself to memories until you got warm and full.

Our kitchen!

What color is soul?
Is it Black like me
Or color free?

Ancestor

Thank God your ancestor,
not then known by his slave name,
crouched low in the ship
bent his back
and grimaced well enough to bear the pain.

Be grateful too that he
did not excuse himself from
the misery of enslavement
but chose to endure
an imprisoned existence.

Was he simply strong in body
or was his mind so sharp
he outwitted those
in charge?

Candidate for Angelhood

I was a candidate for angelhood until someone hollered,
  "The band is in town!"
That's when I kicked off my shoes and threw down my crown

Somebody whispered, "Come go with me"
And I unhooked my wings so I could be free

Next day the angels welcomed me back into the fold
And I promised to follow the rules and do as I was told

So the angels offered me one more chance
But I heard some music and started to dance

The sounds they were playing had so much soul
My feet started moving and I lost control

I twisted my dress, threw up my leg, and then my arm
While the angels stood and looked with such alarm

I was certain they would not consider taking me back
But when I told them I would clean up my act

The angels renewed my membership one more time
And I assured them again that I would tow the line

I was doing just fine until a party started up down the street
When I began to have that same old problem with my feet

I did everything I could to keep my feet still
I tried to stay in place and execute my will

Then I heard somebody shout, "Let's go, I won't tell."
And that's when I decided, "Oh, what the hell."

I had the best time ever. I danced all night long
And begged the band to play one last song

When I came sneaking back to the angeltory late that night
I had a feeling things weren't right

My crown was bent and I had lost one wing
I missed choir rehearsal and wasn't there to sing

The angels shook their heads and said I'd just struck out
I didn't understand what The Angelhood was about

But one angel winked her eye, smiled real wide
And said I would be a fine representative on the outside

So don't feel sorry 'cause I wasn't sad
When they turned me down I was almost glad

Now I will be like my sisters and brothers
I'll just have a good time and be kind to others!

When I woke up this morning, I knew I was alive.
Now I have to prove it to others!

Declare Today

When your mama says, "Get up girl!"
But it's hard for your body to uncurl

And you want to pull the covers over your head
Then say you will get up later instead

Or somebody hollers, "It's time to go, boy!"
And you consider feigning sick could be the ploy

To stay in bed longer, all nice and warm
So you won't have to go out and weather the storm

Choose to get up anyway!
Be glad you have been given another day

Even if you are tempted to sleep some more
Get out of the bed, put your feet on the floor

Declare today the time to make a new stand
To become a better person or do something grand

Start the morning by making a vow
The time is right. The day is now!

Creative Legacy

If Cheops were here...
He would build a great pyramid to mystify the architects
and provide us with an eternal observation

If Beethoven were here...
He would compose a concerto or a symphony
to cause us to revel in the sounds of music

If Tanner were here...
He would paint a canvas with strokes of color and line
to quench our thirst for beauty

If Robeson were here...
He would sing a song with a melody and pitch
to soothe even the refined ear

If Langston were here...
He would write a verse to enhance our appreciation
for the real and the imagined

If Dunham were here...
She would dance a story and make a turn
to stretch our reality of movement

If Dizzy were here...
He would blow a bit of jazz
to make our bodies respond to the rhythm

If Martin were here...
He would preach a sermon or provide an oration
to help us understand the issues of the world

But none are here...
And so we must be the creators who continue their legacies.
They have set the stage and drawn the curtains
inviting us to perform!

Where in the world are you going?
Exactly what is your plan?

_____

Dreamer

There are some people
who barely seem to be alive
They don't know where they are going
or when they will arrive

They wander around looking
and watching others be
Blinded by distraction
and unable to see

They don't comprehend
what life could really mean
They simply are the dreamers
dreaming a dream

How can they be reached
what is it we could do
To help them know they have
a new horizon in their view

For if they follow their dream
and try hard not to veer
They may be lucky enough to discover
why God has placed them here

Reality of Color

Understanding the reality
of your color
is a profound
experience

It unearths the beauty
of self definition
and security

And without apology
allows you to steep
in your culture

You're going too fast for me to catch up,
or is that the plan?

Setting the Cadence

Drrum dum- dum- dumm
Drrum dum- dum- dumm

He was the one out front playing the drum
He knew which way to go and where he had come from

He believed that he could
And planned how he would

He prepared himself so he was ready
And fortified his faith to keep him steady

Some who saw him march down the street
Clapped their hands to help him stay on the beat

Drrum dum- dum- dumm
Drrum dum- dum- dumm

When he arrived he turned to glance
And saw a young brother about to take his chance

He made sure his boots were buckled up tight
And drew him a map so he would go right

While the boy put on his coat and got ready to go
He filled him with the knowledge he had grown to know

Then just to make sure, he struck up the band
And set the little brother's cadence by clapping his hands!

Drrum dum- dum- dumm
Drrum dum- dum- dumm

Drrum dum- dum- dumm
Drrum dum- dum- dumm

Drrum dum- dum- dumm
Drrum dum- dum- dumm

19

Excuse me just a moment please.
I forgot to change my mask.

They Arrived

They arrived, they arrived, they arrived.
They kept arriving!

By the hundreds, by the thousands, by the millions
They arrived!

Cut from the heart of Africa and crowded into the bellies of ships
Stacked for the voyages across the seas

Enslaved on the plantations
Shackled and whipped into obedience to build a future
        for their masters

Escaping through the underground
Then ordered by the Emancipation Proclamation to be elevated
        to noncitizenship

Freed, but unable to vote or participate in the political process
And without the promised 40 acres and a mule

With no civil rights, choice of home, school or job
        to suit their needs
Seated at the back of the bus

Suffering from discrimination, oppression and the humiliation
        of misconception and stereotype

They arrived, they arrived, they arrived.
They kept arriving!

They came, Black men and women
Brilliant, resilient, strong, creative and proud
With minds and bodies of great potential!

Amazing how few were broken and lost their way!

Most arrived to be shopkeepers and teachers,
            inventors and scientists

They arrived to be architects and lawyers,
            homemakers and factory workers

They arrived to be artists and performers,
            physicians and clinicians

They arrived to be builders and designers,
            philosophers and writers

They arrived to be preachers and politicians,
            athletes and astronauts

Both ordinary and extraordinary folks!

They arrived, they arrived, they arrived.
They keep arriving!

Saved

The child went outside where the big boys were
and they told him they had a surprise

He became excited
because he knew they were older and wise

Just at that moment
his mother called from the opened window upstairs

Unaware that she
had just answered her own prayers

The hope for our children is that
they will be wise enough to become who they ought to be
and caring enough to help someone else find their way

Reflections

The same moon that shines
on the homes
with manicured yards,
well-lit walkways
and garages built for two or more cars

That same moon shines
on the garbage-strewn vacant lots
and the stoops of the broken tenements
built with the expectation there would be
no cars needing to be parked

It is the same moon.
But the reflections are different!

If you just let me be, I may not be at all.

Perfect Prayer

She was a beautiful child
and didn't even know
Because in all her life no one
had ever told her so

She listened carefully
to what the others said
And remembered the pictures
in the storybooks she read

No one spoke of her
and she could not recall
A princess or a queen
that looked like her at all

But she was very smart
and each day offered a small prayer
That asked not to be made different,
but simply that she not care.

Eavesdropping . . . It's hard to remain silent
when your conversation is begging for my comment

Will the Real Black American Please Stand

*When identified, please stand and remain standing
until the roll has been completed*

They changed the rules, but you could still play the game

You knew they didn't want you there, but you stayed anyway

They said you couldn't win, but you finished out in front

You sensed there was danger, but you stood to be counted

They said, "Never," and you said, "Now"

Barriers were placed, but you learned to jump higher

They thought they had locked you out, but you found the key

The "For Sale" sign was taken down, but you moved in next door

They said, "Uh uh," and you said, "Mm hmm"

Someone else was given the job, but you found another one

They thought you were down, but you rose back up

You were surrounded by hatefulness, but you had God at your side

They said, "White," and you said, "Try Black"

Is the Real Black American standing? If so, give yourself a hand!

Thank God, most everyone we meet is decent and good. We should remember them instead of those few who are not.

A Story Worth Telling

You are going to have to leave this world some day
And how you are living now will determine what others say

It would be a shame if when you left this earth
When called upon, no one could speak about your worth

Or if folks had trouble knowing what to say
And remembering that you even passed this way

So with a somber face the only thing that could be said
When your obituary was to be read

Is, "It truly is a shame
I only know the date of birth, death and the name"

To make sure this doesn't happen when your time has come
Give them something to recall that you have done

There is still time, your story isn't finished yet
The engraving of the stone has not been set

Decide to write something new
About the plans you have yet to do

That will tell of the life you chose to live
And of all the joy you had to give

The way you worked to make this a better place
To bring a smile to someone's face

Or about all the service you have done
And how you helped others to become

Not concerned about your fame
But that folks smile and speak kindly when they call your name

People sometimes think that just because they are who they are they can do what they do

---

Color Mania

Up here

Down there

Over here   Over there

Everywhere!

There are people who dislike me

They don't know me. We have not met.
We have never even spoken.

They have only **SEEN** me!

You don't know what you don't know
until you know what you know

Grandhoney

At first we tried calling her Grandmother, Nana, and Grandma,
then we tried GRANDHONEY, and that was it!
You didn't even have to explain how sweet she was.
You knew it when you called her name.

When you hadn't done anything to deserve it,
but she hugged you anyway, you'd say, "Thanks,
GRANDHONEY."

When she cooked all day long and you were so full
you had to save some until the next day,
you'd say, "That was s-o-o-o good, GRANDHONEY."

When she rocked you in her arms until you fell asleep and then
put you to bed, you'd look up and say, "Good night,
GRANDHONEY."

When she would hum her gospel songs on the way home
from church on Sunday, you'd say, "Sing, GRANDHONEY."

When she smiled and told you,
"It's going to be all right, sugar" and you knew it would be,
you'd say, "I love you, GRANDHONEY".

Now she has become GREAT GRANDHONEY,
and she is playing her sweet messages,
teaching even more little folks how to turn on their lights.

Kindness is magnetic.
It draws out the best in others.

Passer-by

I was passing by the ghetto one day
And I heard the voice of a small child say

"Please help me build my dream!"

I decided to stop and inquire and I asked the child his name
He said, "It doesn't matter. Our stories are all the same.

"We try to reach up to grab the brass ring,
      but it's moving by too fast
When we get in the race, we've had a late start,
      and so we often finish last."

"Please help me build my dream!"

"There are so many obstacles in the way,
      and our voices are so small
People are rushing and busy and simply don't hear us call

"I often dream and imagine how different my life could be
And of all the ways I could stand and make folks proud of me"

"Please help me build my dream!"

"Some of my friends have given up, but I always knew
Your decision would be to stop one day,
      and so I've been waiting on you."

"Please help me build my dream!"

Winner

If you have a vision
and you know you are doing right

Hold on to your convictions
and keep your goal in sight

There are going to be hurdles
that you will have to leap

And promises may be broken
people said they would keep

But don't let that stop you
from moving straight ahead

Pay no attention
to what other folks have said

Even if someone attempts
to drag you to the side

Stick to your beliefs
and let good judgment be the guide

And when you are almost there
and see the finish drawing near

But feel disappointment because
no one is waiting there to cheer

Just keep right on moving
until the job is done

Then you will have a victory
and be proud that you have won!

Growing Pains

To ease the pain, each child should be given
a daily dose of love and understanding

Note: These should be taken on a full stomach

Childhood Discovery

I could tell you were different by the sound of your name
Yet in many ways we seem much the same

Tell me who you are and how you came to be
Then I can share my culture and help you to know me

What is your favorite food and why do you talk that way
Help me understand the meaning of the words that you say

Explain if you will about your holidays
And why you celebrate in those different ways

Which traditions did your family pass on to you
And what are the special things that you choose to do

Although we realize there are issues on which we don't agree
We could simply decide that you could still be you
        and I could just be me

And celebrate the differences we have discovered
        and maybe in the end
We could demonstrate for others how by respecting
        one another, we can still be friends

What difference should I make about your difference

When the Future Met the Past

The Future met the Past at the crossroads and decided
       to sit a spell
When asked how things were going the Future replied,
       "Not very well."

The Past said, "Explain if you will, why you continue to ignore
And choose to go down the same roads that have been traveled
so many times before

"It seems you haven't learned from the mistakes that already
       have been made
And that you don't remember those who stumbled and the prices
       that they paid

"Why don't you take the time to read your history and recall
What made those in the past fail and what caused them to fall?

"Did you forget the wars that were fought and the reasons why
Humans began to hate, kill and often even die?"

The Past continued, "I would be much smarter if I had the
       opportunity to see
I would make this world a better place for everyone to be

"I would avoid all the same reasons and improve on what
       happened in the past
And make sure that there was peace and harmony
       that could last."

The Future just sat impatiently and didn't say a word
And made no response as if he hadn't heard

Then looked down at his watch and said he was in a hurry
And that he would find his way and told the Past not to worry

So it was they parted, each going their separate way
Perhaps they will have a chance to meet again some day

Maybe the Future will choose not to move so fast
And slow down long enough to learn from the lessons
            of the Past

Sometimes it's hard to enjoy the moment for thinking
of how quickly it will pass

A Windy Happenstance

It was a glorious day when it happened
I remember how hard the wind blew
And how from the very first moment
I was unquestionably sure I knew
The dahlias and daisies were dancing
And the leaves fluttered and twirled
The boughs on the trees were bouncing
Flags flapped and unfurled

Hats on top of heads went flying
Umbrellas were turned inside out
The wind whistled and howled
Forcing passers-by to shout
Folks had their heads bowed so
The wind wouldn't sting their eyes
That's when I bumped into this brother
And discovered the most wondrous surprise

It must have been meant to happen
Because there were many people around
When this brother offered to hold me steady
So the wind wouldn't push me down
I obliged of course, squeezed him tight
And struggled against the wind
And I'd look up and thank him passionately
Every now and then

Far after the wind stopped blowing
We still held on to each other
I whispered a quiet prayer that
Said simply, "Thank you God for this brother."
Here was this man I'd been looking for
Practically all of my life
And had it not been for the wind that day
I wouldn't now be his wife!

Love should be easy to recognize

One Afternoon

We lay quietly side by side
And when we spoke it was with gentle voices
And when we embraced it was warm and comfortable
It went on like that all afternoon

Occasionally a tree branch brushed against the window
And for just a few moments the rain fiercely beat on the rooftop
Then it was quiet again, except for the sounds of love

Friendship

comfortable
supportive
long talks
shared secrets
caring criticism
first to be called
through thick and thin
without pretense
1/2 sandwich or 1/2 dessert
like values
reciprocal
easy

Put That Aside

If thinking of growing old
bothers your soul, just put that aside

Imagine the rainbows you have yet to see
   the snow on the mountains
   the trees standing tall
   flowers opened in bloom
   and the birds flying free!

Picture looking up towards the sky
   the colorful sun
   the moons that hide
   the shining stars
   and the shapes of the clouds that plan to pass by!

If thinking of growing old
bothers your soul, just put that aside

Remember the seasons still to come
   the smell of spring
   the warmth of summer
   the leaves of fall
   and the chill of winter when the year is done!

Celebrate that which has passed and is yet to arrive
   the new baby born
   the folks you have loved
   the friends still on the way
   and you here on earth just being alive!

If thinking of growing old
bothers your soul, just put that aside

I Lied

It was just a prevarication
A simple exaggeration

Just a harmless fabrication
Sprung from my own imagination

I experienced a provocation
When I felt the onset of stagnation

So I thought of a creation
And out came an innocent little **Black** lie!!

Hair

It just isn't right. It simply isn't fair
That a sister has so little control of her hair

You're never really certain of how your hair will be
You just do the best you can, then simply wait and see

You can get started early in the morning way before dawn
Or spend the entire afternoon in the beauty salon

You can press and curl, braid and bend
Or you can choose to let it be natural again

You can mold it, pat it, brush it around
Do everything you can to make the edges lie down

You can choose a new color or a perm to make it straight
But it doesn't really matter, it all depends on fate.

It just isn't right. It simply isn't fair
That a sister has so little control of her hair

There are some days even your very best friend
Will make remarks about the condition your hair is in

I've seen a grown woman cry
And loudly ask the question why

On today of all days
Am I being punished for my ways

I've heard women say, never again
And promise to make Jesus their friend

You see, so much depends on the look of your hair
It doesn't even matter about the outfit that you wear

For if your hair is not looking fine
That two hundred dollar dress can look like nineteen ninety-nine

It just isn't right. It simply isn't fair
That a sister has so little control of her hair

There are probably some who never even knew
A single night's sleep can ruin a beautiful do

Your hair can look gorgeous at night when you go to bed
But when you wake up, it's smashed against your head

Some women have contemplated going to court
When the beautician has cut their hair too short

And then with an attitude proceeded to say,
"In a few weeks your hair is going to look okay."

I've seen women sitting gripped with fear
Worried that the hot iron will brand their forehead or their ear

The worst was when a husband in passion reached out for his
            wife one night
A curler poked him in the eye and he nearly lost his sight

It just isn't right. It simply isn't fair
That a sister has so little control of her hair

Believe me there are times, at least in Seattle
When the mist begins to fall, you know you've lost the battle

Or if the rain should happen to take you by surprise
And your wet hair begins to dry, it is also sure to rise

Sometimes an extension or a wig is the only way
A desperate woman can salvage the day

And if it weren't for hats we would be forced to stay at home
And communicate with folks via the telephone

I tell you all of this because I think you need to know
When you encounter a sister, no matter where you go

Hair can affect her disposition in such a serious way
You have to watch what you do and be careful what you say!

It just isn't right. It simply isn't fair
That a sister has so little control of her hair.

Don't forget to save me a little corner of your heart

My Man

My man deserves a Ph.D.
from the Just Living Institute
He's been there and understands

He has a heap of credits in
Feeling Good and Special Effects

And has obviously taken the
required courses in
Saying The Right Thing

I think I will give him his degree
this Friday night at
my place!

Egocentric Woman

It is my body
> imbedded with my spirit
>> my mind
>> my soul and
>> my keen sense of who I am

I will cherish
> protect
> preserve and
> pamper it

I will exercise
> educate and
> indulge it when I feel the need

I may choose to share it with someone else,
> and then again,

I might decide to keep it all to myself!

Ready To Unfold

Stand back and watch me.
I'm getting ready to unfold!

I've decided to let my spirit go free
I'm ready to become the woman I was meant to be

I've either been somebody's daughter, mother, or wife
And now it's time for me to take charge of my life

I've been pondering all this time trying to decide just who I am
At first I thought it depended on whether I had a man

Then I had the notion that simply just because
Others had more seniority, they could decide who I was

I played all the roles that were expected, and I seldom asked why
I had my wings closed up, but now I'm ready to fly.

I've been awakened, and I finally see the light
I'm about to make some changes and set a few things right

With my new attitude and the knowledge I possess
I may create a whole new world order and clean up all this mess!

Stand back and watch me.
                          I'm getting ready to unfold!

I had so many messages passed on to me, I threw some away. Now I know I should not have been so hasty.

Lookin' Good Lizzy

Lookin' Good Lizzy was wearing that hat!
It was cocked and leaning just off the side of her head.
The color was purple and the feather bright blue,
the kind that bounced when she walked.

Lizzy was stepping in those shoes!
When she walked they shined and dazzled.
It was only the toes and the buckles that glowed,
for the rest of the shoe was soft velvet.

Lizzy looked fine in that dress!
It was fitting around every curve.
With each move of the satin it shimmered,
and the red made a statement that shouted.
This was not a simple dress, and it sure wasn't plain
because it had a big bow and a ribbon.

Lizzy looked good with her head up so high
you knew someone must have told her.
And when she walked in the room a few minutes late
with her purse flung over her shoulder

The music stopped playing and folks turned around
And just for a moment there wasn't a sound

Maybe it was the clothes, who really knows
what exactly was the cause
But when Lizzy placed her hands on her hips
and puckered her lips, folks broke into applause!

Talking About Religion

I like to talk about my religion, 'cause I sure 'nuff got it!

I go to church every Sunday and to prayer meeting too
My religion is with me in everything I do

When I sing in the choir, I can blend in on any chord
I'm the best usher they have on the board

I take my religion wherever I go
And I talk about it all the time in case folks don't know

I like to talk about my religion, 'cause I sure 'nuff got it!

When I tell folks about my religion and how righteous I am
They have expressions on their faces like they don't understand

Their eyes get all wide with a look of dismay
And they act as though they don't believe what I have to say

So I tell them again how religion is suppose to be
And point out the fine characteristics in me

Some have said I was unchristian like, but it must be those few
Who have not seen me every Sunday sitting in the same pew

I like to talk about my religion, 'cause I sure 'nuff got it!

When I find one or two who have not yet seen the light
I make sure they know the difference between wrong and right

I can quote from the scripture word for word
And there aren't too many sermons that I haven't heard

Just in case one day our preacher should slip and fall
Folks have my number and know that I'm on call!

I like to talk about my religion, 'cause I sure 'nuff got it!

Transform your good intentions.

The Great Reunion

Mahalia was all by herself making an ordinary hymn have new meaning. You could feel the spirit! Then Marian walked in, poised herself and listened only for a moment before adding her deep melodic sound. It made you stand to attention!

Bessie and Billie heard the music and invited themselves to join in the song. It wasn't the same after that. They added the blues to what was already soulful. It made you want to shout, cry or just be still and quiet so you could feel it all over! You might say it was a sophisticated spiritual filled with soul, or you could call the sound they made an elegant rendition of the blues.

But after Ella's late arrival you didn't know what to say it was. When she started scatting in the background with Sarah, it made you tingle and raise your hand like you were fixing to testify.

They sang and sang. And then after a while they started up again.

It was a great reunion!

Every now and then it may be helpful to look down
and check your color
just to make sure you know what others are seeing.

Remember When

Do you remember when you were just a chile
And the simplest of pleasures would cause you to smile

When she was just a girl not so long ago
Happiness is all she thought there was to know

He remembers when he was but a boy
And it took so very little to bring him joy

But that was then and this is now
And things seem to have changed somehow

The world is turning
But folks quit learning

To do unto others as you would have them do to you
That's an old lesson and it sure ain't new

Yet folks forgot when they grew up
And started drinking from a different cup

Do you remember when it was all right for us to disagree
Well times ain't like they used to be

You hardly had to worry and there was little need to fear
When we lost our way or directions were unclear

Why have things not stayed the same
And where can we find to place the blame

Days go on and years pass by
And now we ask the question why

The world is turning
But folks quit learning

To do unto others as you would have them do to you
That's an old lesson and it sure ain't new

Yet folks forgot when they grew up
And started drinking from a different cup

Do you remember no matter what and no matter when
A friend was a friend until the end

Why have things changed this way
How did love and kindness seem to slip away

There must be a way to create peace
To cause our hatred and anger to cease

I don't know how and I don't know when
But if I could I'd start all over again

The world is turning
But folks quit learning

To do unto others as you would have them do to you
That's an old lesson and it sure ain't new

Yet folks forgot when they grew up
And started drinking from a different cup

Do you remember when?

The Basics

Love
Food
Shelter
Clothing
Peach Cobbler

Journey, So Far

It's been a marvelous journey, so far!

We've had to kick some fairly large stones from the road and
        often maneuver a sharp turn
And even back way up to start again when the pathway has been
        hard to discern

Sometimes we've been forced from the road to let
        some others pass by
And had to sit on the side with our heads hung down so folks
        wouldn't see us cry

It's been a marvelous journey, so far!

Because since we started this life God has been traveling
        with us each day
So we've been able to explore and venture to the edge,
        yet still find our way

When we've fallen, we've gotten up again, because God has been
        right above
Yes, we've had joy in our travels and even found folks
        we could love

It's been a marvelous journey, so far!

Now we've gotten rid of some baggage so we're traveling light
And we've learned to read directions to find the path that is right

Our journey ahead is still considerable, we know
But if we keep God as our compass, we'll know which way to go

It's been a marvelous journey, so far!

Did you notice the sunshine keeps following you?